how2become.com

CSSE ESSEX 11+ TEST: ENGLISH

In-depth Revision & Sample Practice Questions for the 11+ English Essex Grammar School Test

www.How2Become.com

As part of this product you have also received FREE access to online tests that will help you to pass your eleven plus (11+) assessments.

To gain access, simply go to:

www.MyEducationalTests.co.uk

Get more products for passing any test at:

www.How2Become.com

Orders: Please contact www.How2Become.com

ISBN: 9781911259893

First published in 2017 by How2Become Ltd.

Copyright © 2017 How2Become.

All rights reserved. Apart from any permitted use under UK copyright law, no part of this publication may be reproduced or transmitted in any form or by any means, electronic or mechanical, including photocopying, recording, or any information, storage or retrieval system, without permission in writing from the publisher or under licence from the Copyright Licensing Agency Limited. Further details of such licenses (for reprographic reproduction) may be obtained from the Copyright Licensing Agency Ltd, Saffron House, 6-10 Kirby Street, London EC1N 8TS.

Typeset by Gemma Butler for How2Become Ltd.

Printed and bound by CPI Group (UK) Ltd, Croydon, CR0 4YY

Disclaimer

Every effort has been made to ensure that the information contained within this guide is accurate at the time of publication. How2Become Ltd is not responsible for anyone failing any part of any selection process as a result of the information contained within this guide. How2Become Ltd and their authors cannot accept any responsibility for any errors or omissions within this guide, however caused. No responsibility for loss or damage occasioned by any person acting, or refraining from action, as a result of the material in this publication can be accepted by How2Become Ltd.

The information within this guide does not represent the views of any third party service or organisation.

CONTENTS

- An Introduction to the Guide ... 8

CHAPTER 1:
REVISION TIPS FOR PARENTS ... 9

- Revision Tips for Parents ... 10

CHAPTER 2:
USEFUL HINTS AND TIPS ... 13

- Useful Hints and Tips ... 14

CHAPTER 3:
LITERARY TERMS AND TECHNIQUES ... 17

- Literary Terms and Techniques ... 18

CHAPTER 4:
THE STRUCTURE OF THE TEST ... 23

- The Structure of the Test ... 24

CHAPTER 5:
COMPREHENSION PRACTICE QUESTIONS AND ANSWERS ... 27

- Comprehension Practice Questions 1 ... 28
- Answers to Comprehension Practice Questions 1 ... 37
- Comprehension Practice Questions 2 ... 41
- Answers to Comprehension Practice Questions 2 ... 50
- Comprehension Practice Questions 3 ... 53
- Answers to Comprehension Practice Questions 3 ... 61

CHAPTER 6:
APPLIED REASONING PRACTICE QUESTIONS AND ANSWERS 65

- Applied Reasoning Practice Questions 1 66
- Answers to Applied Reasoning Practice 1 68
- Applied Reasoning Practice Questions 2 69
- Answers to Applied Reasoning Practice 2 71
- Applied Reasoning Practice Questions 3 72
- Answers to Applied Reasoning Practice 3 73

CHAPTER 7:
CONTINUOUS WRITING PRACTICE QUESTIONS AND ANSWERS 75

- Continuous Writing Practice Questions 1 76
- Answers to Continuous Writing Practice 1 79
- Continuous Writing Practice Questions 2 81
- Answers to Continuous Writing Practice 2 83
- Continuous Writing Practice Questions 3 85
- Answers to Continuous Writing Practice 3 87

CHAPTER 8:
FINAL ADVICE 89

- Final Advice 90

An Introduction to the Guide

The consortium of selective schools in Essex requires you to take **two** tests (one **English**, one **maths**) in order to gain entry into any of the following **ten** schools:

1. Colchester County High School for Girls.
2. Colchester Royal Grammar School.
3. King Edward VI Grammar School.
4. Shoeburyness High School.
5. Southend High School for Boys.
6. Southend High School for Girls.
7. St. Bernard's High School for Girls.
8. St. Thomas More High School for Boys.
9. Westcliff High School for Boys.
10. Westcliff High School for Girls.

In this book we will be focusing on the **English** part of the exam. This book is designed to help you practise the skills needed in order to pass. It will also provide you with an assortment of example questions, similar to those that you will face in the real exam. Furthermore, we will provide you with some useful hints and tips to help you prepare for the assessment.

There is also another book in this series, based on the type of questions that you will have to answer in the Maths paper.

*Please note that the questions within this book are designed to give an <u>idea</u> of the <u>types</u> of questions that will be asked in the CSSE 11+ exam. These example questions will not correlate exactly to the questions that children will be required to answer on the real paper.

CHAPTER 1: REVISION TIPS FOR PARENTS

Revision Tips for Parents

- While it is the school's responsibility to prepare your child for their upcoming exam, support and encouragement from parents can go a long way. Encouraging your child to do even a small amount of practice outside of school can really improve their performance.

- Do not overload your child with stacks of work. This will only make them feel overwhelmed and discourage them. As with many things, it is best to break up their revision sessions into small, manageable chunks. This will ensure that their concentration levels remain high, and that they are able to take in the information that is being covered.

- Following on from the last point, make sure you schedule in plenty of rest breaks for your child. Allow them to go outside or participate in an activity that they enjoy doing. This boosts their energy and prepares them for the next time they sit down to study.

- Reward their progress and achievements. This doesn't have to mean anything extravagant, but when they have done well, or mastered a certain type of question that they had been struggling with, a small reward will make it all feel worthwhile.

- Have key notes or definitions placed around your home or your child's bedroom. This will refresh the memory subliminally and help small portions of information to sink in. Visual aids are a great way to stimulate a child's brain.

- Encourage your child not to feel embarrassed about discussing topics that they don't understand, so that they are able to talk through them.

- Plan to focus on a specific topic in each 'session'. This will ensure that revision is not too overwhelming. Begin with a topic that they find the most challenging, and interchange this with a topic that they are confident on – this will keep their confidence at a stable level.

- Encourage note-taking and bullet-point making. If your child is simply reading through questions and working them out in their head, they are less likely to retain key information.

REVISION TIPS FOR PARENTS

- Make sure your child has an environment to study in which is as distraction-free as possible. Ideally, you should choose somewhere not too noisy or cluttered. This will also mean that they will get more done, as they can avoid potential interruptions.

- Similarly, when your child has set aside some time to revise, make sure that the television is off, there are no phones available, and the focus is purely on the subject at hand. This means that once it is time for a break, these things will serve as a reward for them in their free time.

- Once your child has become confident with a certain type of question, try encouraging them to practise under timed conditions. They do not necessarily have to do a whole past paper in one sitting, but even just one timed section will help to simulate the feel of the actual exam day.

- Gradually build up to longer sessions. If your child is having trouble concentrating, start with short twenty-minute sessions and aim to build them up over the course of their exam preparation. This makes a lot more sense than sitting your child down for an hour or two and expecting them to stay concentrated from the outset.

- It may sound obvious, but make sure your child is getting enough sleep. If you haven't already, try and establish a solid routine. This will mean that they are able to concentrate and retain more information.

- It is especially important to try and ensure that your child gets adequate sleep the night before the exam. Try not to make them feel too stressed or pressured in the evening, and reassure them that you are confident in their abilities. This will alleviate some of the worrying that can occur in the days leading up to the exam.

- Let your child know that you are proud of them – whatever the outcome. They do not need the added pressure of worrying about potential failure. The best thing you can do is to encourage them.

- Getting the right nutrition is also essential for everything from concentration, to sleep, to mood. Ensure that your child is eating healthily and has a well-balanced diet. Consuming too much sugar or high-fat foods will make your child's energy levels peak and then crash, thus negatively affecting their performance.

- Similarly, make sure your child is getting plenty of fresh air and exercise. They should be spending a small amount of time outside each day. This will also keep their concentration levels high and help them to get a refreshing sleep every night.

- Try not to leave revision to the last minute. This will only make your child feel unnecessarily stressed and anxious. If you start introducing small, manageable bites of revision a good amount of time before the exam, it will make for a much more productive outcome in the long run.

In summary, we recommend positively encouraging your child, plus helping them to revise gradually and progressively over time. It's also extremely important that you aim to increase their confidence. Make sure they are getting everything they need at home, such as a comfortable environment to study in and a well-balanced diet, and reward them for their achievements.

We wish you and your child the best of luck in their exams!

CHAPTER 2:
USEFUL HINTS AND TIPS

Useful Hints and Tips

- The CSSE Essex 11+ exam is designed specifically to test what you learned in your Key Stage 2 English lessons. Therefore, it is important to brush up on all the key skills you have been working on at school, as well as trying your hand at some example practice questions, such as those covered in this book. This also includes an array of literary skills, which we will discuss in the next chapter.

- If you don't read already, try doing some reading in your spare time. Try a book from your school or local library, and read a little before bed each night or after school. This will help you greatly with the comprehension part of the exam, as will be explained later on in this book.

- The examiners will be assessing the way in which you answer the questions in your English exam, so make sure you pay attention to the details of your answers. Take care to ensure that they are as clear and accurate as possible. This includes making sure all words used are spelled correctly, and that the correct punctuation is used.

- With the previous point in mind, it is also crucial that you understand what each question is asking before you start to answer it. Re-read a question if you are unsure.

- Make sure you allocate your time in the exam wisely. Whilst it is important to make sure you understand and spend enough time on each question to get the best marks, you don't want to end up rushing any questions at the end of the paper.

- When you are given your test paper, it will have recommended amounts of time to spend on each section of the exam. Whilst these times are only given as a guide, bear in mind that they have been formulated to try and help you make the most of your time, so try to stick to them wherever possible.

- The amount of marks that can be awarded for each question will be given in the margins of the test paper. This should also be an indicator for how long you should be spending on each question. Generally speaking, the higher the amount of marks you are able to get, the longer you should be spending answering the question.

USEFUL HINTS AND TIPS

- If you get really stuck on a question, don't spend too long thinking about it. Instead, move on to answering the rest of the paper to the best of your abilities, and leave some time at the end to come back and re-visit any questions that you were unsure about the first time around.

- The exam board recommend that where you are asked to choose from a list of different responses, (i.e. multiple-choice questions), ensure that you always choose the one that you feel is the *most appropriate*.

- Make sure you practise all of the different types of questions before the exam. If there are certain types of questions you find harder to answer, or topics you struggle with, spend a little more time practising them.

- Try answering some of the example questions in this book under timed conditions. This will prepare you for the actual exam environment.

CHAPTER 3: LITERARY TERMS AND TECHNIQUES

Literary Terms and Techniques

As mentioned before, the questions you will be asked in the exam will be testing the knowledge you have gained throughout your English studies at school. The questions require an understanding of things such as:

- Similes;
- Metaphors;
- Alliteration;
- Word Definitions;
- Prefixes and Suffixes;
- Synonyms and Antonyms;
- Homophones;
- Spelling;
- Grammar and Punctuation.

Make sure you have a basic understanding of these things, so that you know how best to make use of them yourself, and spot them in passages of text for the highest marks.

For example, the last section of the exam calls for you to do some independent writing, where you will be marked on your use of words, spelling, grammar and punctuation. You will also score well if you can spot and make use of some of the literary techniques, which we will go over in further detail in this book.

Below is a list of common literary techniques that you may come across or be expected to look out for during the exam. Have a look and see how many of them you recognise. We have given a brief definition of each one to refresh your memory.

Allegory – stories in which the characters represent abstract ideas or qualities.

Alliteration – repetition of first consonant sounds such as 'beautiful baby boy'.

Hyperbole – a wild exaggeration, such as 'I am so hungry, I could eat a horse'.

LITERARY TERMS AND TECHNIQUES

Iambic Pentameter – ten-syllable lines of poetry, of which every other syllable is stressed.

Imagery – descriptions of sight, sounds, touch, taste and smell.

Metaphor – a figure of speech that identifies something as being the same as another, unrelated thing, such as 'The road was a ribbon of moonlight'.

Satire – work that makes fun of something or someone.

Simile – drawing parallels or comparisons between two things, such as 'I was cold as an ice cube'. Often denoted by using the words 'as' or 'like'.

Onomatopoeia – use of words that sound like what they mean, such as 'buzz', 'bang'.

Oxymoron – a phrase that is made up of two opposite words, such as 'organised chaos'.

Personification – giving human characteristics to an inhuman object, such as 'the car accelerated, enraged.'

Pun – the use of a word that plays on multiple meanings.

Irony – language that conveys certain ideas, by saying the opposite.

You may recognise some or all of these techniques from your school studies. Now that you have had a brief reminder of what each of them mean, have a go at constructing a sentence or two for each definition below. We have left you space to write your own short example for each.

Allegory:

Alliteration:

Hyperbole:

Iambic Pentameter:

Imagery:

Metaphor:

Satire:

Simile:

LITERARY TERMS AND TECHNIQUES

Onomatopoeia:

Oxymoron:

Personification:

Pun:

Irony:

It is also useful to keep your eye out for these techniques when you are reading. Doing so would be very good practice for the English exam, during which you may be required to identify the techniques from a passage of text you have been given. As well as this, you may have to use them yourself in other parts of the exam.

CHAPTER 4: THE STRUCTURE OF THE TEST

The Structure of the Test

The English test will be divided into **three** main sections:

1. Comprehension.
2. Applied reasoning.
3. Continuous writing.

You are given a total of **one hour and ten minutes** to complete the exam.

Here is a quick breakdown of what each of these sections consist of, and how the exam board recommends you utilise your time.

Comprehension

This section requires you to read a passage or an extract of text, and subsequently answer a range of questions based upon what you have just read.

For the real exam, it is recommended that you spend approximately **ten minutes** reading the extract given, and a further **thirty minutes** answering the related questions.

The lines of the text will be numbered in order for you to be able to refer back to them when giving your answers.

The types of questions that you will be asked in the comprehension section are designed to test your understanding of the text and the words and themes within it. They will be a combination of both multiple choice and longer, more descriptive questions.

Applied Reasoning

It is recommended that you spend **ten minutes** on this part of the test in the real exam. During this section, you will be asked a few different types of 'verbal reasoning' style questions.

Given the time frame you have to answer these questions, you will have to complete them fairly quickly. They will involve more 'quick fire' type exercises and they will be prefaced with an example question and answer, so that you can get an idea of what the question is asking of you.

Continuous Writing

You will be given a separate booklet for this part of the test. It is recommended that you spend around **twenty minutes** completing this section in the real exam.

You will be set a couple of tasks, and then asked to write a number of sentences (around six or seven) on a subject or topic in your own words.

It makes sense to divide your time evenly for these two questions, so with that in mind you should aim to spend around **ten minutes** answering each one.

For these questions, you will be assessed on the creativity and quality of the pieces you write, along with the correct and proper usage of punctuation and spelling.

CHAPTER 5: COMPREHENSION PRACTICE QUESTIONS AND ANSWERS

Comprehension Practice Questions 1

As we mentioned before, in this part of the exam it is advised that you spend around **ten** minutes reading the extract given to you, and then a further **thirty** minutes answering the questions that follow. Have a look at our example questions and see if you can answer them under timed conditions, after spending about ten minutes reading the extract. This will help you get to grips with the structure of the exam.

Remember, you can refer back to the extract as many times as you need to.

Bear in mind that you are likely to see a few words you might not be entirely familiar with, but just try and interpret the text to the best of your ability.

There are *40 marks* available in total for this section.

Have a read of the short passage of text below, and take a look at the questions that follow:

P1. Mimi sighed audibly as she trudged her way through the grassy, marshy fields. The sky was as drab and uninspiring as her father's journey playlist. Even the trip there felt never-ending. Why did her family insist on dragging her to these tragically monotonous events? They didn't even give her a choice, branding her as 'anti-social' if she didn't attend every single one.

P2. *I'm hardly social when I'm here anyway*, she thought. *I just plug my headphones in and try desperately to imagine I'm somewhere at least vaguely more compelling, with enthralling company. Or even on my own, for that matter.*

P3. She failed to see the point of these strangely optimistic, elated people – all oddly beaming at each other – trying to coax someone, anyone, into purchasing decrepit pieces of furniture and long-discarded hand-me-downs for a pitiful sum.

P4. "One day you'll understand, Mimi," her mother would say, "One day you'll stop being a miserable teenager and realise all the incredible treasures just waiting to be uncovered, and appreciate all the wonderful, joyful people to chat to."

Mimi disagreed. No matter how old and dull she became, she would never find the thought of dragging herself through stalls of musty clothes and rusty trinkets thrilling. Did people seriously think it was realistic to find anything of any discernible value at these kinds of events?

P5. Her parents would try and excite her by recalling stories of folk who purchased some inconspicuous knick-knack, only to find out later that it was worth millions and would instantaneously change their lives forever. They would march about the never-ending fields, her father whistling to himself joyfully, and her mother on an overly optimistic and frankly misguided mission to discover some unbelievable hidden gem.

P6. *At least I've got Toby here with me,* Mimi thought, *My one small source of joy and amusement.* On this occasion, however, Toby wasn't being particularly well-behaved. Although a loyal companion, he had never responded particularly well to any kind of training. He would often tug on the lead when taken for walks with the family, dragging his poor owners along with him, and then stop abruptly and root himself to a spot at other times, refusing to move.

P7. Toby's obedience had long been an issue that the family had tried hard to overcome, yet no matter what they tried, he seemed hell-bent on doing whatever he could to resist any kind of training. Mimi caught a glimpse of her dad – stumbling, staggering, sweating – being hauled along mercilessly by Toby. For the first time in the day she cracked a slight smile, and almost started to snigger. She suddenly realised what she was doing and quickly reverted to the unimpressed, slightly overcompensating, wanton expression – just to make sure no one thought that she was actually enjoying herself.

P8. Mimi decided to put her dad out of his misery and offered to take Toby's lead, so that her parents could continue rummaging around the stalls. *See, I am a thoughtful daughter,* she thought to herself. *I'm never actually appreciated for these kinds of gestures.*

"Be careful with him Mimi, he's very energetic today," her dad warned. "I know Dad - I think I can handle it," Mimi retorted sarcastically. She soon realised her dad's caution was not to be scoffed at, as Toby proceeded to drag her from right to left, forcing her to increase her pace to a tremendously tumultuous jog within seconds of taking the lead.

P9. Mimi had soon lost sight of her parents. Before she knew it, she was being bustled through stall after stall, occasionally knocking something off a rail or a table. She heard a few angry voices shout "Oi!" or "Come back here!" but she didn't dare to turn around for fear of getting tangled in Toby's lead, or worse, losing him completely. Her parents wouldn't forgive her if she let him run off. Her mum would definitely be 'mortified' and most certainly 'die from embarrassment' as she often proclaimed to do, even after the most minor of situations.

COMPREHENSION

Questions

(*40 marks* available in total for this section)

Question 1

Who is Toby? *(1 mark)*

a) Mimi's father.

b) Mimi's brother.

c) The family dog.

☐

Question 2

What kind of event are Mimi and her family attending? *(1 mark)*

a) Music festival.

b) Boot fair.

c) Barbeque.

d) Sporting event.

☐

Question 3

Identify some clues from the passage which show the event that Mimi and her family are attending. *(3 marks)*

_____

_____

_____

Question 4

a) Find an example of a SIMILE in the text. *(1 mark)*

b) Describe what this simile means. *(1 mark)*

Question 5

List **four** words or phrases from the extract that demonstrate Mimi's *negative* response towards her surroundings. *(4 marks)*

-
-
-
-

Question 6

In paragraph **7**, 'stumbling, staggering, sweating' is used within a sentence. What literary technique is being utilised here? *(1 mark)*

a) Metaphor.

b) Simile.

c) Irony.

d) Alliteration.

e) Allegory.

[ ]

Question 7

Find another example of the literary term referenced in **question 6** within the text. *(1 mark)*

_____

Question 8

Describe **two** ways in which Mimi's parents speak *positively* about the fair. *(2 marks)*

- _____

  _____

- _____

  _____

Question 9

In paragraph **7**, what does the writer mean when they say that Toby is 'hell-bent' on resisting training from his owners? *(2 marks)*

_____

_____

_____

Question 10

Why does Mimi choose to do an 'overcompensating wanton' expression in paragraph **7**? *(2 marks)*

_____

_____

_____

Question 11

What does Mimi mean when she says she will 'put her Dad out of his misery' in paragraph **8**? *(2 marks)*

_____

_____

_____

Question 12

Which **two** words within the text most strongly imply that Mimi does not believe that her mother will find anything valuable at the fair?
(2 marks)

a) Inconspicuous.

b) Optimistic.

c) Unbelievable.

d) Misguided.

e) Amusement.

[   ]

Question 13

What is it that makes Mimi start to laugh? (1 mark)

a) Her parents believing that they can find something valuable.

b) Toby dragging her dad around.

c) Mimi's dad warning her of Toby's behaviour.

Question 14

Which of the following words best describes people's reaction to Mimi accidentally knocking things over? (1 mark)

a) Irate.

b) Curious.

c) Confused.

d) Regaled.

c) Enthusiastic.

Question 15

'She soon realised her Dad's caution was not to be scoffed at'. Paragraph **8**. What does Mimi mean by this? (2 marks)

_____

_____

_____

CSSE ESSEX 11+ TEST: ENGLISH

Question 16

Within the given passage, find **one** phrase or word which most closely resembles the phrase or word on the left. Next to each question there is an indication as to which paragraph to focus your search on.

(13 marks)

• Swamp-like	_____	P1
• Everlasting	_____	P1
• Beguiling	_____	P2
• Ecstatic	_____	P3
• Noticeable worth	_____	P4
• Despondent	_____	P4
• All of a sudden	_____	P5
• Reject	_____	P6
• Ruthlessly	_____	P7
• Malevolent	_____	P7
• Mockingly	_____	P8
• Unrestrained	_____	P8
• Interlaced	_____	P9

Answers to Comprehension Practice Questions 1

(<u>40 marks</u> available in total for this section).

Q1. C - The family dog. *(1 mark)*

Q2. B - Boot fair. *(1 mark)*

Q3. Mention of fields in paragraph 1.

In paragraph 3 Mimi talks of people who try and sell old furniture for money.

In paragraph 4 Mimi's Mum talks of finding treasures there.

In paragraph 4 Mimi talks of the 'stalls' old clothes and 'trinkets' and it's mentioned that people think they can find something of value.

In paragraph 5 Mimi's parents talk of people finding something and selling it on for a large sum of money and 'hidden gems'.

Paragraph 8 mentions rummaging around stalls.

In paragraph 9 Mimi knocks items off stalls and rails.

You should mention at least 3 key points and expand on them slightly. *(3 marks)*

Q4.

a) "The sky was about as drab and uninspiring as her father's journey playlist". *(1 mark)*

b) The weather was bad, grey, overcast etc. similar to the way in which her father's music choices were dull (or similar response).

(1 mark)

Q5.

Permitted responses:

- Drab;
- Uninspiring;
- Tragically;
- Monotonous;
- Decrepit;
- Musty;
- Rusty;
- Dull. *(4 marks)*

Q6. D – Alliteration. *(1 mark)*

Q7. 'Tremendously tumultuous'. *(1 mark)*

Q8.

- They believe there are valuable items to be found and speak of people who have made a lot of money from selling on things they have bought at these types of events;
- Her mother talks of the lovely people there are to talk to at the fair.

(2 marks)

Q9. The writer means that Toby is trying desperately to do anything possible to sabotage the training his owners have imposed upon him. He is determined, at all costs, to be disobedient. *(2 marks)*

Q10. Mimi is trying to hide the fact that she smiled. She does not want anyone to think she is happy or enjoying herself and thus she does an 'overcompensating' and 'wanton' expression in order to cover her smile. *(2 marks)*

COMPREHENSION 39

Q11. She means that she will take Toby. This will 'put her dad out of his misery' because Toby is disobedient and therefore Mimi's dad is struggling to control him. By Mimi offering to take the lead she intends to make it easier for her dad. *(2 marks)*

Q12.

B – Optimistic.

D – Misguided. *(2 marks)*

Q13. B – Toby dragging her dad around. *(1 mark)*

Q14. A – Irate. This means 'annoyed' and 'angry'. *(1 mark)*

Q15. She means that she should not have mocked her dad's warning about Toby, as she soon realises that his behaviour is actually very difficult to handle. *(2 marks)*

Q16.

- Swamp-like ⇨ 'Marshy'
- Everlasting ⇨ 'Never-ending'
- Beguiling ⇨ Accept 'compelling' or 'enthralling'
- Ecstatic ⇨ 'Elated'
- Noticeable worth ⇨ 'Discernible value'
- Despondent ⇨ 'Miserable'
- All of a sudden ⇨ 'Instantaneously'
- Reject ⇨ 'Refusing'

- Ruthlessly ⇨ 'Mercilessly'
- Malevolent ⇨ 'Wanton'
- Mockingly ⇨ 'Sarcastically'
- Unrestrained ⇨ 'Tumultuous'
- Interlaced ⇨ 'Tangled'

(13 marks)

Comprehension Practice Questions 2

Again, have a look at the passage of text below, and try answering the questions within the time frame you would be given in the real exam (**ten** minutes reading and **thirty** minutes answering the related questions).

Remember, you can refer back to the extract as many times as you need to.

There are *40 marks* available in total for this section.

P1 All year he's been tormenting me. In fact, I can't actually remember a time where I haven't woken up feeling physically sick at the thought of the abuse that I would be subjected to that day. Even at the weekend the thoughts spiralled endlessly through my mind. All the things he had said to me that week, to everyone else around me – the humiliation.

P2 It's bad enough on a 'normal' day, but sports day is fast approaching, and my anxiety has well and truly peaked this weekend. If I fake one more injury the suspicions will be too high. It's not like they can prove anything though, right? If I twist my ankle whilst running I twist my ankle whilst running. So what if it's happened twice already? In reality, the law of probabilities doesn't actually make it any less likely to happen this time around just because it's happened before. As a matter of fact, it might actually be more likely, because clearly, I have some kind of functional problem with my left ankle. I should probably get that checked out.

P3 The thing is, I'm just way too much of an awkward person to do it again. I'm not a good liar. I know I'm not. As soon as I've made my claim, I get so extraordinarily paranoid that someone might see me walk normally for one step, or question me just a bit too much to the point where I end up giving in and ashamedly admitting to exactly what it is I've done. Then he'd abuse me even more. I wouldn't hear the end of that.

P4 The words don't come out the same when I'm lying. As soon as I start to lie, people gain this unnatural ability to be able to see right through me. I become transparent. They start piecing together all the reasons why I might be faking it (one in particular) and that's when the doubt comes creeping into their minds.

P5 No, I can't do it this time. I vividly remember feeling extremely on edge even last year. It's not worth the risk of having them find me out, and then him find me out, and then even more cruelty being flung my way. I have to just knuckle down and participate. That's it then, I'm doing it. I'm going to have to get through the whole day without being taken off to the safe and secure nest of the injury gazebo. He couldn't get me there and even if he tried then he would be told to move on and leave me alone. But no, I can't get away with it again.

P6 It wouldn't be as bad if I wasn't participating in all the same events as him. Why did they even pick me for long jump? My legs are about as short as the trees they had severed into stumps last year to make the place brighter. Just means less places to hide for me. No, I'm almost certain I get picked for long jump every year because they enjoy watching me suffer at the hands of my bully. Everyone knows he's my bully, and not only do they not do anything about it, I'm convinced that it's all a conspiracy, and I'm actually just a morbid source of entertainment for the staff.

P7 As if long jump wasn't bad enough, they've actually put me forward for shotput this year. Shotput. If this was the Olympics we'd be bottom of the leader board with these kinds of preposterous selections. The fact that they have chosen me for shotput honestly just confirms my suspicions that they actually enjoy my suffering. If I don't get a heavy ball to the head, I'd be very much surprised. I can see it coming already. He'll claim it was an accident, and that he let go of the ball at the wrong time. He's so sorry. Still, at least that would mean I could sit the rest of it out I suppose.

P8 I think the worst part of it all, worse than having to put up with the fear every evening, worse than enduring the pain every day, was the fact that I have never understood why he has it in for me. What have I done to deserve it? I must have been a menace to society in a past life to have to tolerate this kind of treatment in my current one. It's the fact that no one quite gets it either. I've given up telling my mum; her advice is honestly more frustrating than anything else. "Rise above it, Jimmy", she says, "Just ignore him". Okay thanks Mum, really practical stuff. I wish she would just move me to a different school, or have me home-schooled or something. Imagine that. Waking up every day and not even having to leave the house. Just safe in the little bubble of home.

P9 I better start psyching myself up. I need to do it for longer than I do for my everyday routine. I'm going to have a lot more to contend with tomorrow than usual. Can't let him see my fear this time. Can't let him have the pleasure of knowing that I've been dreading this day all year. I'm just going to act completely nonchalant, as if I haven't even given it a second thought. I'll just get my activities out the way, and try and find a hideaway somewhere. I've already scoped out the situation and have a few places in mind. I can do this.

Questions

(*40 marks* available in total for this section).

Question 1

Is the main character worried that he might have a problem with his ankle? Explain your answer in three or four sentences. (Paragraph **2**). *(3 marks)*

_____
_____
_____
_____
_____
_____

Question 2

What does Jimmy worry about being found out about in paragraph **3**? *(1 mark)*

a) That he doesn't want to participate in sports day.

b) That he is faking an injury.

c) That he cheated at sports day.

d) That he is an awkward person.

COMPREHENSION 45

Question 3

Find an example of alliteration in paragraph **3**. *(1 mark)*

_____

Question 4

Explain in your own words what Jimmy means when he says, "I become transparent" in paragraph **4**. *(2 marks)*

_____

_____

_____

Question 5

In paragraph **5**, who does Jimmy think will find him out? Write **two** answers. *(2 marks)*

- _____

- _____

Question 6

What does the expression "knuckle down" refer to in paragraph **5**? *(1 mark)*

a) Jimmy getting involved in the sports day activities to the best of his abilities.

b) Jimmy punching his bully.

c) Jimmy faking an injury to his ankle to get out of sports day.

☐

CSSE ESSEX 11+ TEST: ENGLISH

Question 7

Find an example of a SIMILE in paragraph **6**. *(1 mark)*

_____

Question 8

What is meant by this simile? *(1 mark)*

_____
_____

Question 9

Explain what Jimmy means when he says that he thinks him being chosen for long jump is a "conspiracy". Use evidence from paragraph **6** in your answer. *(3 marks)*

_____
_____
_____
_____

Question 10

Why does Jimmy think that they would perform badly if they were at the Olympics? See paragraph **7**. *(2 marks)*

_____
_____
_____

COMPREHENSION 47

Question 11

In paragraph **7**, what positive outcome does Jimmy foresee if his bully hurts him with the shotput? *(1 mark)*

a) He will be able to tell on him.

b) He won't have to participate in the rest of sports day.

c) His bully will get in trouble.

☐

Question 12

"I never understood why he had it in for me". Paragraph **8**. What does Jimmy mean by "had it in for me"? *(1 mark)*

_____

_____

Question 13

Jimmy states in paragraph **8** that he must have been a "menace to society in a past life". Explain, in three or four sentences, what you think he means by this. *(3 marks)*

_____

_____

_____

_____

_____

Question 14

In paragraph **8**, Jimmy says his mother's advice isn't helpful. Why is this? *(2 marks)*

_____

_____

_____

Question 15

Jimmy states that he needs to start "psyching himself up" before sports day in paragraph **9**. What does he mean by this? *(2 marks)*

_____

_____

_____

Question 16

What does Jimmy mean when he says that he has already "scoped out" the situation in paragraph **9**? *(2 marks)*

_____

_____

_____

Question 17

Within the given passage, find **one** phrase or word which most closely resembles the phrase or word on the left. Next to each question there is an indication as to which paragraph to focus your search on.

(12 marks)

- Upsetting   _____   P1

- Ceaselessly   _____   P1

COMPREHENSION 49

- Likelihoods _____ **P2**
- Confessing _____ **P3**
- Atypical _____ **P4**
- Tense _____ **P5**
- Morose _____ **P6**
- Absurd _____ **P7**
- Anguish _____ **P7**
- Put up with _____ **P8**
- Exasperating _____ **P8**
- Blasé _____ **P9**

Answers to Comprehension Practice Questions 2

(*40 marks* available in total for this section).

Q1. No, he is not worried he has a problem with his ankle. In paragraph 2 he states he should "probably get that checked out" but he is being *sarcastic*. This is because he says that he has faked having problems with his ankle on past sports days to get out of participating in the events. *(3 marks)*

Q2. B – That he is faking an injury. *(1 mark)*

Q3. 'Ashamedly admitting'. *(1 mark)*

Q4. He means that people are able to tell that he is lying. They can 'see through' his lies just as you are able to see through something that is transparent. *(2 marks)*

Q5.
- The teachers;
- His bully. *(2 marks)*

Q6. A - Jimmy getting involved in the sports day activities to the best of his abilities. *(1 mark)*

Q7. "My legs are about as short as the trees they had severed into stumps last year". *(1 mark)*

Q8. He is comparing the length of his legs to tree stumps, implying that they are not very long. *(1 mark)*

Q9. He means that he thinks his teachers have a scheme in which they have chosen him on purpose. Jimmy believes that this is because he says that "everyone knows he's my bully" but they still chose him. He believes that the reason the staff are doing this is because it is a "morbid source of entertainment" for them. *(3 marks)*

Q10. He thinks that they would perform badly if they were at the Olympics because the people they have selected for certain sporting activities have not been particularly suitable for them. He refers to himself having been chosen to participate in shotput and long jump. *(2 marks)*

Q11. B - He won't have to participate in the rest of sports day. *(1 mark)*

Q12. Jimmy means that he didn't understand why his bully targeted him in particular over anyone else. *(1 mark)*

Q13. He is talking about the belief that if you are suffering in this life it must be because of something bad you have done in a past life. Therefore he is alluding to the thought that he must have done something bad, i.e. been a "menace to society" in his past life and his punishment in this life is the fact that he is being constantly bullied at school. *(3 marks)*

Q14. His mum gives advice that he thinks is not "practical". He thinks that she, like others, does not understand the severity of the problem and that therefore the things she says to him do not actually help or change the situation in any way. *(2 marks)*

Q15. He means that he needs to prepare himself mentally for sports day. This is because he needs to be equipped for what his bully could do to him. *(2 marks)*

Q16. He means that he has assessed the place that the sports day is being held. He is talking about the fact that he has found areas where he thinks he can hide from his bully. *(2 marks)*

Q17.

- Upsetting ⇨ 'Tormenting'
- Ceaselessly ⇨ 'Endlessly'
- Likelihoods ⇨ 'Probabilities'
- Confessing ⇨ 'Admitting'
- Atypical ⇨ 'Unnatural'
- Tense ⇨ 'On edge'
- Morose ⇨ 'Morbid'
- Absurd ⇨ 'Preposterous'
- Anguish ⇨ 'Suffering'
- Put up with ⇨ Accept 'enduring' or 'tolerate'
- Exasperating ⇨ 'Frustrating'
- Blasé ⇨ 'Nonchalant' *(12 marks)*

Comprehension Practice Questions 3

Have another go at reading the extract in **ten** minutes, and answering the questions in **thirty** minutes.

Remember, you can refer back to the extract as many times as you need to.

There are *40 marks* available in total for this section.

P1 My city. The beautiful backstreets bustle, and the gorgeous alleyway aroma drifts and flows and fills my nostrils, as I scamper, satisfied, along the cold stone pavements. I feel a rush of warmth inside of me as I catch glimpse of my friends. I see their nude tails whip violently, excitedly, around the corner and I scurry to catch them. To be reunited once again with Todd, Marsha, George and oh…there's my brother, Harry. The gang all together again, like it should be.

P2 We all pause for a moment to catch precious breath and I look up at the people above. They look empty, like hollow marching clones, clumping and thumping their enormous bodies around, drifting aimlessly into one brightly lit shop after another. I strain my eyes staring for so long in a seemingly timeless daze that yellows and reds and blues start to merge into one strange aura of colour and light, and I lose all awareness of the commotion around me.

P3 I don't think I will ever tire of living here. At least that's one thing I can be sure of. As for my friends, I eventually snap myself out of my hazy restful state to find that they have completely deserted me. Not to worry, I think, I'm fine here on my own at the moment. I do seem to have a habit of losing myself in my own thoughts, only to find that everyone else has already long gone.

P4 As I continue to make my way down the street, I decide to have a bit of fun. I start to dodge in and out of people's feet and legs, even sometimes accidentally brushing my tail gently against them. This makes them scream with terror. Sometimes they jump up and run away, and I watch them as they disappear into the distance. I really don't know what it is about me that induces such a reaction, but I guess bigger isn't always better. I rule this city. No doubt.

P5 I quickly dart back into the familiar alley to escape from the people's voices. The drones, the piercing laughter, it is all starting to get a bit much for me. Dinner. What's on the menu tonight? Every night is a surprise for me, I can tell you that! No ordering and waiting for hours on end, no deliberating over this and that. No, I'm not a time waster. Life is too short, as they say. I know, I know – it's a cliché but it's entirely true. At least in my opinion. Got to experience everything you possibly can, meet people. I cross paths with the type of personalities that spark my imagination in this city every single day.

P6 Finding something to eat proves more difficult than it sounds tonight. To be honest it does seem to be getting a lot tougher as of late. All I want is something small, just to tickle my stomach. Although I wouldn't say no to a warm, hearty meal – haven't had one of those in a while. Still, I go on. Must be the early hours of the morning by now. The city never sleeps, eh? Well I certainly do. I delight in curling up in the deliciously pungent sewer.

P7 I pick my favourite spot to settle down and find Marsha and Todd already resting close by. We eventually all fall asleep to the disappointed rhythms of our empty, rumbling stomachs. Sounds like they haven't had much luck with dinner tonight either.

P8 Within minutes of drifting off, the intense pang in my stomach wakes me again. This sort of thing seems to be turning into a routine just lately. The pain is sharper than usual this time, and every muscle in my body feels tired and sore. I plead with myself just to relax and drift back into sleep for probably an hour, to no avail.

P9 I decide to have a bath to try and ease the aches and pains and help me relax a little more. I indulge in a thick, warm bath in one of my favourite corners of the sewer. I admittedly feel a little better but as soon as I step out I realise that the relief was short-lived. I eventually give in and decide that I will have to force myself up and head back into the city on another mission for nutrition.

P10 I should probably have asked my friends to come with me this time. Many hands make light work as they say. I didn't want to wake them, though, and I'm not sure where my brother or George are. I'll probably end up bumping into them in one of our usual spots. The trouble for us is that people seem to be throwing away less and less. The streets are tidier and the bins are emptier. It may be a nicer environment for the humans – but do they ever think of how it affects us?

COMPREHENSION 55

Questions

(*40 marks* available in total for this section).

Question 1

What literary technique is made use of numerous times in paragraph 1? *(1 mark)*

_____

Question 2

Find three examples of this technique in paragraph **1**, and write them below: *(3 marks)*

- _____
- _____
- _____

Question 3

Why has the author used this technique in the text, and what impact does it have upon the feel of the piece? *(2 marks)*

_____

_____

_____

Question 4

What literary technique is made use of in **line 3** of paragraph **2**? *(1 mark)*

_____

Question 5

"*I lose all awareness of the commotion around me.*" Select which two of the below words are synonyms for the word 'commotion'.
(2 marks)

a) Tumult.

b) Scarcity.

c) Filth.

d) Disorder.

e) Disagreements.

f) Poverty.

Question 6

Take a look at paragraphs **3**, **4** and **5** and select which of the following statements are true. Choose **two** statements: *(2 marks)*

a) The main character doesn't like his home.

b) The people in the story are scared of the main character.

c) The main character retreats, as the street becomes too noisy.

d) The main character has a very specific taste in food.

e) The main character's friends deserted him because he was annoying them.

Question 7

Find **three** clues in the text that give you an idea of what kind of creature the main character is, and write them below. *(3 marks)*

• _____

- _____
- _____

Question 8

"The city never sleeps, eh?" (Paragraph 6) What does the protagonist mean by this statement? *(2 marks)*

_____

_____

_____

Question 9

"Sounds like they haven't had much luck with dinner tonight either". *(Paragraph 7)*. How does the main character know that his friends haven't had dinner? Give an example from the text in paragraph **7**.

(2 marks)

_____

_____

_____

Question 10

Give at least **two** examples from the text which demonstrate the fact that it is not certain whether or not the characters will eat dinner each night. Why is this the case? *(4 marks)*

_____

_____

_____

_____

Question 11

Does the main character manage to get back to sleep? Find one phrase in the text in paragraph **8** to prove your answer. *(1 mark)*

Question 12

"*The relief was short-lived*". *(Paragraph 9)* Explain what is meant by this statement and write your answer in the context of the events in paragraph 9. *(3 marks)*

Question 13

"*Many hands make light work, as they say*". *(Paragraph 10).* What does the protagonist mean by this comment? *(2 marks)*

Question 14

Find **three** examples from the text in which the main character speaks positively regarding his environment. *(3 marks)*

COMPREHENSION 59

Question 15

Within the given passage, find **one** phrase or word which most closely resembles the phrase or word on the left. Next to each question there is an indication as to which paragraph to focus your search on.

(9 marks)

- Contented　　　　_____　　**P1**

- Valuable　　　　　_____　　**P2**

- Brings about　　　_____　　**P4**

- Shrill　　　　　　 _____　　**P5**

- Weighing up　　　_____　　**P5**

- Candid　　　　　　_____　　**P6**

- Twinge　　　　　　_____　　**P8**

- Respite　　　　　　_____　　**P9**

- Customary　　　　_____　　**P10**

Answers to Comprehension Practice Questions 3

(*40 marks* available in total for this section).

Q1. Alliteration. *(1 mark)*

Q2.

"Beautiful backstreets bustle".

"Alleyway aroma".

"Flows and fills".

"Scamper, satisfied". *(3 marks)*

Q3. It draws the reader's attention to the description of the city and helps the text to flow. It makes the piece easier to read and grabs attention from the start. It enhances the description of the opening scene, creates a rhythm and helps to set the mood. *(2 marks)*

Q4. Onomatopoeia. *(1 mark)*

Q5.

A – Tumult.

D – Disorder *(2 marks)*

Q6.

B - The people are scared of the main character.

C - The main character retreats as the street becomes too noisy.

(2 marks)

COMPREHENSION

Q7.

"Scamper".

"Nude tails whip".

"Dodge in and out of people's feet and legs".

"Brushing my tail".

"I delight in curling up in the deliciously pungent sewer".

"One of my favourite corners of the sewer".

"It may be a nicer environment for the humans - but do they ever think of how it affects us?" *(3 marks)*

Q8. He means that there is always something going on in the city – shops and bars are always open and people are out and about at all hours of the night and day. *(2 marks)*

Q9. He knows that they haven't had dinner because he hears their stomachs making noise signifying this: *"We all fall asleep to the disappointed rhythms of our empty, rumbling stomachs".* *(2 marks)*

Q10. It is down to luck whether or not they have dinner, because they have to find what they can when they can, due to the fact that they are animals who scavenge for food.

In paragraph 5, the main character says: "What's on the menu tonight? Every night is a surprise for me".

Later on in the text, in paragraph 6, he explains that "Finding something to eat proves more difficult than it sounds".

He also says in paragraph 6: "To be honest it does seem to get be proving a lot tougher as of late" and later mentions that he hasn't had a "hearty meal" for a while.

He notices that his friends "haven't had much luck with dinner tonight either", in paragraph 7.

In paragraph 9, he states that he must go on another "mission for nutrition".

"The trouble for us is that people seem to be throwing away less and less. The streets are tidier and the bins are emptier. It may be a nicer environment for the humans - but do they ever think of how it affects us?" This implies that it will be less likely than it used to be that they find something to eat.

You must include at least **two** relevant examples such as these from the text, and also a short explanation. *(4 marks)*

Q11. The main character does not manage to get back to sleep. This is demonstrated when he states that he tried desperately to get back to sleep "to no avail". *(1 mark)*

Q12. It means that the relief from the bath didn't last for long. He said he felt better at first, but as soon as he got out he felt bad again. *(3 marks)*

Q13. He is talking about how he should have asked his friends to help him find food, because the more people that can help, the easier and quicker a task will be to perform. *(2 marks)*

Q14. "The beautiful backstreets bustle and the gorgeous alleyway aroma drifts and flows and fills my nostrils".

"I don't think I will ever tire of living here".

"I cross paths with the type of personalities that spark my imagination in this city every single day".

"One of my favourite corners of the sewer". *(3 marks)*

COMPREHENSION

Q15.

- Contented ⇨ Satisfied
- Valuable ⇨ Precious
- Brings about ⇨ Induces
- Shrill ⇨ Piercing
- Weighing up ⇨ Deliberating
- Candid ⇨ Honest
- Twinge ⇨ Pang
- Respite ⇨ Relief

Customary ⇨ Usual *(9 marks)*

CHAPTER 6: APPLIED REASONING PRACTICE QUESTIONS AND ANSWERS

Applied Reasoning Practice Questions 1

Remember, in the real exam you are advised to spend approximately **ten minutes** on this section. Below are some practice questions to get you used to the kind of things you may be asked. Once you have understood what the question is asking of you, you can try having a go at answering the sets of questions under timed conditions.

There are 5 *marks* available in total for this section.

Give one letter which completes the end of the first word, and begins the start of the second word. You must use the same letter for both words,

For example:

you (r) ate   pea (r) ain

By finding just one letter, you can see that it ends the first word in the sequence and is the start of the second one. The result is that there are now **four** new words formed: your, rate, pear and rain.

Question 1

tim (?) ase   sur (?) arl   *(1 mark)*

Question 2

car (?) ove   lar (?) oor   *(1 mark)*

Again, give one letter which completes the following words. This time the letter may be at the beginning, the end or in the middle of the words. For example:

sa (n) d   (n) otice

As you can see, this question is similar to the one above, in that you have to find one letter in common that both of the words are missing. The only difference here is that the missing letters can be anywhere within the word, not just at the beginning or end.

Question 3

pi (?) (?) a   (?) ebra *(1 mark)*

Question 4

fon (?)   s (?) a (?) ion *(1 mark)*

Now use the letters within the word '**mother**' to make **four** other new **four letter words.** You can use the letters in any order you wish.

For example, **mote** uses the four of the letters within the word **mot**her to form a new word.

Question 5: *(1 mark)*

List five **four-letter** words that you can make from the word '**mother**' below:

- _____
- _____
- _____
- _____
- _____

If you can complete questions one to five in approximately ten minutes, then it will be very useful in preparing you for this section of the real exam. Check your answers afterwards to see if you are on track, and go back and focus on any that you didn't quite understand the first time around. Then have a go at the other two example practice sections.

Answers to Applied Reasoning Practice 1

(<u>5 marks</u> available in total for this section).

Q1. E – Forming the words time, ease, sure and earl. *(1 mark)*

Q2. D – Forming the words card, dove, lard and door. *(1 mark)*

Q3. Z – Forming the words pizza and zebra. *(1 mark)*

Q4. T – Forming the words font and station. *(1 mark)*

Q5. Any from the following:
- hero;
- home;
- more;
- mote;
- moth;
- term;
- them;
- tome;
- tore. *(1 mark)*

APPLIED REASONING

Applied Reasoning Practice Questions 2

There are *5 marks* available in total for this section.

The below words are missing **three** letters each. All the missing letters have the same pattern.

The pattern is: the second missing letter is **three** letters along in the alphabet from the first one.

After that, the third missing letter is **four** letters along in the alphabet from the second one.

For example:

(?) (?) n (?) gn   *is completed as*   (b) (e) n (i) gn

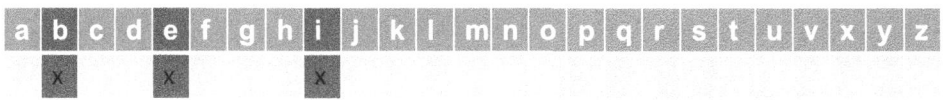

Now try the completing the following in the same way, using the alphabet chart to help you.

Question 1

con (?) (?) r (?)   *(1 mark)*

Question 2

(?) (?) cker (?)   *(1 mark)*

Question 3

(?) bse (?) (?) e   *(1 mark)*

CSSE ESSEX 11+ TEST: ENGLISH

The words below can be completed in a number of different ways. Once you have chosen the two letters to make two different words, use these two letters to form another separate word.

For example:

s (?) ade   s (?) ade   (?) o (?) e

Should be filled in as:

s (**h**) ade   s (**p**) ade   (**h**) o (**p**) e

As you can see, the letters **h** and **p** form the words 'shade' and 'spade'. The two letters **h** and **p** then fit into the next gaps to form the word 'hope'. See if you can complete the questions below using the same method.

Question 4

har (?)   har (?)   o (?) ene (?)   *(1 mark)*

Question 5

co (?) e   co (?) e   co (?) (?) ert   *(1 mark)*

APPLIED REASONING

Answers to Applied Reasoning Practice 2

(*5 marks* available in total for this section).

Q1. con (**f**) (**i**) r (**m**)   *(1 mark)*

Q2. (**l**) (**o**) cker (**s**)   *(1 mark)*

Q3. (**o**) bse (**r**) (**v**) e   *(1 mark)*

Q4. har (**p**)   har (**d**)   o (**p**) ene (**d**)   *(1 mark)*

Q5. co (**n**) e   co (**v**) e   co (**n**) (**v**) ert   *(1 mark)*

Applied Reasoning Practice Questions 3

There are *5 marks* available in total for this section.

The below words are missing **three** letters each. All the missing letters have the same pattern.

The pattern is: the second missing letter is **two** letters along in the alphabet from the first one.

After that, the third missing letter is **four** letters along in the alphabet from the second one.

For example:

(?) oyal (?) (?)   *is completed as*   (**r**) oyal (**t**) (**y**)

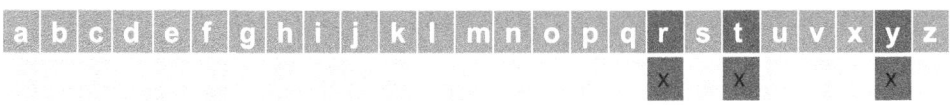

Now try completing the following in the same way, using the alphabet chart to help you.

Question 1

p (?) u (?) ge (?)   *(1 mark)*

Question 2

c (?) n (?) (?) er   *(1 mark)*

Question 3

(?) r (?) at (?) on   *(1 mark)*

Question 4

b (?) (?) klo (?)   *(1 mark)*

Question 5

(?) ran (?) is (?)   *(1 mark)*

Answers to Applied Reasoning Practice 3

(*5 marks* available in total for this section).

Q1. p (**l**) u (**n**) ge (**r**) (*1 mark*)

Q2. c (**o**) n (**q**) (**u**) er (*1 mark*)

Q3. (**c**) r (**e**) at (**i**) on (*1 mark*)

Q4. b (**a**) (**c**) klo (**g**) (*1 mark*)

Q5. (**b**) ran (**d**) is (**h**) (*1 mark*)

CHAPTER 7: CONTINUOUS WRITING PRACTICE QUESTIONS AND ANSWERS

Continuous Writing Practice Questions 1

In the exam, you will be advised to spend around **twenty minutes** on this section. You will be asked to write independently, and your work will be assessed on the creativity and quality of the piece. In addition, correct and proper usage of punctuation and spelling will be important.

You are generally advised to write about six or seven sentences for each question, so you should try to stick roughly within this limit. As mentioned before, it makes sense to divide your time equally between the two questions, therefore spending around **ten minutes** on each one.

On the following pages, we have provided you with some space to practise writing your own answers to our example questions. As with the practice questions before, make sure you understand what the question is asking, and try to have a go at timing yourself when you write your answer.

There are *15 marks* available in total for this section.

CONTINUOUS WRITING

Question 1

In six or seven sentences, write a description of a woodland scene. Try to make it as imaginative as possible.

Question 2

Give instructions on how best to clean your room in around six to seven sentences. Make sure your instructions are clear and include as much detail as possible.

Answers to Continuous Writing Practice 1

Remember, for these questions, you will be assessed on how well you write. The examiner will be looking closely at your **spelling**, your **punctuation**, and the way in which you make use of and **structure** your words and sentences.

For this reason, there is no clear marking scheme in terms of a right or wrong answer. Each answer is assessed as a piece in its own right, and judged on its **quality** and **originality**.

As well as making sure you are careful with your spelling and punctuation, take a look at some of the **literary terms and techniques** at the beginning of the revision guide and see if you can make use of any of them in your answer. This will prove to the examiner that you understand these techniques, and how to use them, as well as making your piece of writing interesting and compelling to read. Remember, however, that you won't be rewarded for simply throwing these techniques in, or trying to use as many as possible. There need to be a clear reason for why you are using each technique, so make sure you use them sensibly.

Focus mainly on the quality of your piece rather than trying to fill up the text boxes you are provided with in the answer booklet. It will be obvious to the examiner if you are writing in order to use up space rather than focusing carefully on each word and creating a captivating piece of text.

Let's have a look at how you *could* go about answering the practice questions in this book. Remember that there are no right or wrong answers.   (*15 marks* available in total for this section)

Q1.

(In six or seven sentences, write a description of a woodland scene. Try to make it as imaginative as possible.)

You want to make the examiner feel as though they could really imagine themselves in the scene you are describing.

Try including **imagery, or sensory descriptions**: what does it look like there? What does it smell like? What sounds are there? By explaining these things, you are painting a picture in the examiner's mind of what it would feel like to actually be in the woodland scene.

Try and include a few **literary techniques**. When you are using these, see if you can be creative. The examiner is looking for something original and different. Similes, metaphors and alliteration are all great techniques to make use of in these kinds of questions.

Q2.

(Give instructions on how best to clean your room in around six to seven sentences. Make sure your instructions are clear and include as much detail as possible.)

For this question, it makes sense to think more about the **structure** before you begin your answer. If you plan this at the beginning, even if it's just quickly in your head, it will ensure that your piece of writing flows well. This is very important when composing your piece, as you don't want it to appear disjointed and confusing.

Think about how **you** would clean **your** room. Maybe you'd throw everything onto the bed and do it from there, or maybe you'd start by organising things into categories, and then spend time on each section one after the other.

Go into **detail** with your answer. Try not to say something you think would be too predictable. If you can think of an interesting or new kind of way to tidy, go ahead. The examiner wouldn't want to read hundreds of papers all giving the same type of description. If you can, try and think of at least one small thing to make your piece **original**.

Continuous Writing Practice Questions 2

There are *15 marks* available in total for this section.

Question 1

Describe in detail your favourite pet, or a pet you would like to own. Explain your reasons, and try to make your description as detailed as possible. Aim to write around six or seven sentences.

Question 2

In about six or seven sentences, write instructions as to how to pack a picnic bag. Try and make your descriptions as clear and detailed as possible.

Answers to Continuous Writing Practice 2

Remember there are no right or wrong answers here, just advice on how to compose a compelling piece of text.

(*15 marks* available in total for this section).

Q1.

(Describe in detail your favourite pet, or a pet you would like to own. Explain your reasons, and try to make your description as detailed as possible. Aim to write around six or seven sentences.)

Do you notice the way in which this question is similar to the previous practice question, about describing a woodland scene? Both questions are asking you to put together a detailed and interesting **description** of something, and, as such, you can take a somewhat similar approach.

With this in mind, think again about including some very detailed descriptions of the animal you choose. **Imagery**, or **sensory descriptions** would be a great thing to include in your answer to this question. Think about all the smaller details of what the animal looks like, and what noises it makes.

How does the animal move? Perhaps think about **personifying** the animal (describing its human-like attributes) to make your description even more compelling. Imagine that the examiner has never seen the animal you are describing before.

This question is asking you **why** this animal is your favourite. Try and give a few good reasons, as if you are trying to **persuade** the examiner why this animal is a great one to choose.

Again, it is always useful to try and include a few **literary techniques**. As before, be creative with the ones you use, as well as how and where you use them.

Q2.

(In about six or seven sentences, write instructions as to how to pack a picnic bag. Try and make your descriptions as clear and detailed as possible.)

Do you notice how this question is in a similar format to the previous one, asking to give instructions on how to clean your room? Both are asking you to describe **how** to do something in a step-by-step manner.

For this reason, it is again important to think about the **structure** of your answer before you begin writing. Think about all the foods you would include and how you would prepare them, and in what order. For example, softer foods may have to be packed last, as they will otherwise get squashed.

Explain **why** you have chosen each item and go into detail with your answer. Make your answer as original and interesting as possible.

CONTINUOUS WRITING

Continuous Writing Practice Questions 3

There are *15 marks* available in total for this section.

Question 1

Describe, in detail, your perfect day out. Write around six to seven sentences.

Question 2

Write around six to seven sentences explaining how to play your favourite game. Try and make you answer as informative and detailed as possible.

Answers to Continuous Writing Practice 3

Again, bear in mind there are no right or wrong answers for this, but here is some advice on how you can create an interesting piece:

(*15 marks available in total for this section*)

Q1.

(Describe, in detail, your perfect day out. Write around six to seven sentences.)

This is another question asking you to write a detailed **description** of something.

Once you have thought about which day out you are going to write about, you should include some details about what you would do on the day, and again include **imagery**. What would you smell there? What can you see? What can you hear or is it incredibly quiet?

Again, imagine you are trying to **persuade** the examiner that this is the best day out to choose. Try and make use of at least one or two **literary techniques** in your answer, to give some depth and interest to the piece.

Q2.

(Write around six to seven sentences explaining how to play your favourite game. Try and make you answer as informative and detailed as possible.)

This question calls for another step-by-step guide on **how** to do something. Starting from the beginning, choose your favourite game and write down the process of how to play it.

Is there anything you need to set up for it? What would be suitable to wear? Is it an active game which requires a warm-up?

How do you play the game? Imagine you are describing it to someone who has never played it before.

Again, focus your attention on the **structure** of your answer and try to be as detailed as possible in your descriptions of what you need to do.

CHAPTER 8: FINAL ADVICE

Final Advice

You have now come to the end of the book for CSSE 11+ Test CSSE Essex 11+ Test: English. In-depth Revision & Sample Practice Questions for the 11+ English Essex Grammar School Test.

Now you are well prepared for the types of questions you will be asked in the exam.

- To recap, the English test will be broken down in the following way:

> **Part One**: **Comprehension**: 10 minutes reading time of the extract you are provided with, and 30 minutes answering the questions in the answer booklet.
>
> **Part Two**: **Applied Reasoning**: 10 minutes to answer the verbal reasoning questions in the answer booklet.
>
> **Part Three**: **Continuous Writing**: 20 minutes to answer the questions given in a *separate* answer booklet.

- When you are given your exam paper on the day of the test, make sure to read through all the information at the front and carefully fill in your details. You will be given time to do this before you begin the exam.

- The front of the exam paper will break down the timings and basic instructions, so you can always refer back to this if you forget anything during the exam.

- Make sure you write your answers clearly in the answer booklets provided.

- Remember, when going through this revision guide, keep trying any questions you didn't quite understand, and check the answers to see if you are on the right track.

- Make sure you brush up on your literary techniques as mentioned in the beginning of this book. This will help you to be able to spot them in texts, as well as make use of them yourself.

- Have a go at practicing some of your answers under timed conditions, so that you are used to the feel of the timings on the exam day.

We wish you the best of luck in your English exam!

WANT MORE HELP WITH THE CSSE 11+ TEST?

CHECK OUT OUR OTHER REVISION GUIDES:

FOR MORE INFORMATION ON OUR REVISION GUIDES, PLEASE CHECK OUT THE FOLLOWING:

WWW.HOW2BECOME.COM

Get Access To

FREE

11+ Tests

www.MyEducationalTests.co.uk

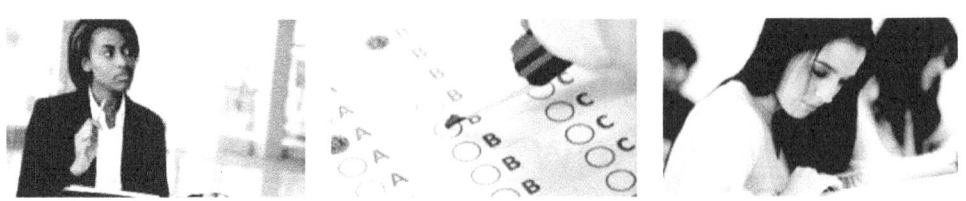